Braveheart

John D. Clare

HODDER
EDUCATION

AN HACHETTE UK COMPANY

The Publishers would like to thank the following for permission to reproduce copyright material:
Photo credits p.5 © Icon/LaddCo/Paramount/The Kobal Collection; **p.10** © Corbis Sygma; **p.11** all © Corbis Sygma; **p.16** The Royal Collection © 2008 Her Majesty Queen Elizabeth II; **p.18** © 2008 The British Library; **p.19** © Bettmann/Corbis; **p.21** © Colour History; **p.23** © 2008 The British Library; **p.25** © Rischgitz/Getty Images; **p.26** t © Corbis Sygma, b © Mary Evans Picture Library 2008; **p.27** © Corbis Sygma; **p.28** t © UK City Images/Topfoto, b © Icon/LaddCo/Paramount/The Kobal Collection; **p.29** tr © Lebrecht Music & Arts, ml © Bettmann/Corbis, br © Stirling Smith Art Gallery and Museum; **p.30** t 'Surrounded by armed men, Wallace was taken to Westminster Hall to be tried as a traitor', illustration from 'Heroes & Heroines of English History' by Alice S. Hoffman (colour litho), Browne, Gordon Frederick (1858–1932) (after)/Private Collection/The Bridgeman Art Library, b © Andrew Hillhouse; **p.31** r © Corbis Sygma, l © Mary Evans Picture Library 2008; **p.32** © Mary Evans Picture Library 2008; **p.37** © The British Library 2008; **p.39** t The Trial of Sir William Wallace at Westminster, Scott, William Bell (1811-90) (att. to) © Guildhall Art Gallery, City of London/The Bridgeman Art Library, b © Ray Roberts/Alamy; **p.40** © Douglas McCarthy/Mary Evans Picture Library; **p.41** © Stirling Smith Art Gallery and Museum; **p.43** © Darren Banks/Rex Features; **p.47** © Icon/LaddCo/Paramount/The Kobal Collection; **p.48** © Stephen Hird/Reuters

Acknowledgements p.4 Extract from The Corries, 'O flower of Scotland', reprinted by kind permission of Ronnie Browne; **p.10** Extract from Sharon Krossa, Regarding the Film Braveheart (2001); Script extract from Randall Wallace, Braveheart (1995); **p.11** Cartoon re-drawn from David Webster, This is Scotland (Oban Press, 1964); **pp.17, 20** Extracts from J.D. Mackie, A History of Scotland (Penguin Books, 1978), copyright © J.D. Mackie, Geoffrey Parker and Bruce Lenman, 1978, reprinted by permission of Penguin Books Ltd; **p.33** Extract from Allan Burnett, William Wallace and All That (Birlinn, 2006), reproduced by permission of Birlinn Ltd www.birlinn.co.uk.
Every effort has been made to trace all copyright holders, but if any have been inadvertently overlooked the Publishers will be pleased to make the necessary arrangements at the first opportunity.

Although every effort has been made to ensure that website addresses are correct at time of going to press, Hodder Education cannot be held responsible for the content of any website mentioned in this book. It is sometimes possible to find a relocated web page by typing in the address of the home page for a website in the URL window of your browser.

Hachette UK's policy is to use papers that are natural, renewable and recyclable products and made from wood grown in sustainable forests. The logging and manufacturing processes are expected to conform to the environmental regulations of the country of origin.

Orders: please contact Bookpoint Ltd, 130 Milton Park, Abingdon, Oxon OX14 4SB. Telephone: (44) 01235 827720. Fax: (44) 01235 400454. Lines are open 9.00–5.00, Monday to Saturday, with a 24-hour message answering service. Visit our website at www.hoddereducation.co.uk

© John D. Clare 2009
First published in 2009 by
Hodder Education,
An Hachette UK Company
338 Euston Road
London NW1 3BH

Impression number   5 4 3 2 1
Year   2013 2012 2011 2010 2009

Cover photos: Peers and commoners fighting, © 2008 The British Library, Bronze statue of William Wallace © David Gowans/Alamy
Illustrations by Tony Jones, Tony Randell and Richard Duzczak (cartoons)
Typeset in Imperial 11/13.5pt by Lorraine Inglis Design
Printed in Italy

A catalogue record for this title is available from the British Library

ISBN: 978 0340 957 714

Contents

Singing the same song?

For centuries, the peoples of England and Scotland have been rivals, not all of it friendly, and some of it downright bloody. That rivalry has affected the words of the national anthems we still sing today. The National Anthem of the United Kingdom, for instance – as well as asking God to save the Queen – also asks Him to crush the 'rebellious Scots'! Equally, however, Scotland's unofficial 'national anthem' celebrates the Scottish 'War of Independence', when the Scots kicked the English out of Scotland.

SOURCE 1

Lord grant that Marshal Wade
May by thy mighty aid
Victory bring.
May he sedition hush,
And like a torrent rush,
Rebellious Scots to crush.
God save the Queen!

The sixth verse of the British National Anthem.

Marshal Wade was the English general who kept Scottish rebels under control after the 1715 rebellion.

SOURCE 2

O flower of Scotland
When will we see your like again
That fought and died for
Your wee bit hill and glen
And stood against him
Proud Edward's army
And sent him homeward
Tae think again.

'O Flower of Scotland' – Scotland's unofficial national anthem.

'Proud Edward' is the English King Edward II, who was defeated at the Battle of Bannockburn, 1314.

William Wallace

Almost no certain facts are known about William Wallace. He arrives as if out of nowhere in 1297, wins a battle, and is made Guardian of Scotland. He sends a letter to the merchants of the German trading town of Lübeck, loses a battle, resigns and in 1305 is captured and executed.

Everything else you thought you knew is either questionable, doubtful … or downright wrong. It all comes from the stories of English or Scottish chroniclers of the time – and they were openly biased. The source that tells us most about Wallace is a fifteenth-century poem called *The Wallace*, which was *perhaps* written by a minstrel called Blind Harry (who may not have been blind). It is mostly myth and much of it can be proved to be wrong.

There are two places – maybe three – where Wallace might have been born. We do not know what he looked like, we cannot say how old he was, and we do not have a clue what he thought about it all. Very few facts, over a career of just eight years. Yet one modern Scottish writer has said of Wallace:

'*Wallace is the darling of ordinary Scots. He is the abiding figurehead of Scotland itself.*'

David R Ross, speaking in 2005.

William Wallace was there at the start of the Scottish War of Independence, and his memory has affected England-Scotland relations ever since. He is Scotland's hero, and this book will ask you to consider whether he deserves to be.

SOURCE 3

Mel Gibson played the part of William Wallace in the film *Braveheart* (1995).

Activities

1. Do the Scots and the English *really* hate each other?
2. Suggest a caption for Source 3 (above).
3. Write down your 'First thoughts on William Wallace': what does he mean to you?

CHAPTER 1

Braveheart

Interpretations: William Wallace – cinema-style

The movie *Braveheart*, screened in 1995, was a huge success. It took more than $200 million worldwide, and the American news channel CNN puts the film's sequence on the Battle of Stirling Bridge in the top ten best film battles of all time. It tapped into Scottish pride, and some people claim it was the reason why, in 1997, the Scottish people voted to set up their own Parliament.

The film is almost entirely fictional, full of errors, and loosely based on the fifteenth-century poem *The Wallace*, by Blind Harry – which itself was mostly myth. But *Braveheart* has created our modern ideas of what the Scottish War of Independence was all about.

This is the story that *Braveheart* told:

In AD 1280, Edward I of England – 'a cruel pagan known as Longshanks' – invites the nobles of Scotland to a meeting, where he treacherously murders them all (William Wallace, still a boy, discovers their bodies hanging in a barn). William's father and brother leave their rough highland croft to go to fight Longshanks, but both are killed. At their funeral, William is comforted by a little girl, Murron, who gives him a thistle.

Having been educated abroad by his uncle, William returns as a mature man and begins to repair his croft. Longshanks's soldiers have been ruling Scotland harshly, but William wants nothing but peace. In a Celtic ceremony, he marries Murron – secretly, to avoid the English custom of *primae noctis* (the right of a lord to sleep with every bride on her wedding day).

Things go wrong when English soldiers try to rape Murron, and William fights them off. As a punishment for the fight, the English sheriff cuts Murron's throat. William returns, kills the sheriff and burns the English castle. Thousands of Scots join him and revolt against the English. Other rebels join Wallace, including Stephen, a mad Irishman who calls Ireland: 'my Ireland'.

At the 'Battle of Stirling', Wallace 'picks a fight' with the English. He inspires the frightened Highlanders and then shows them how to use long spears (which he has invented) to defeat the English cavalry. The English are defeated. Wallace invades England, captures York, and sends Longshanks the head of its military commander in a basket.

Edward I is a psychopath. He throws his son's gay lover from a window, and declares that his greatness will be known when Scotland lies in ashes. He sends his son's wife (Isabelle of France) to talk with Wallace – when, secretly, he is shipping Irish soldiers to Scotland. Angry that she has been made a liar, Isabelle warns Wallace, and he returns to Scotland to fight the English.

At the battle of Falkirk, Stephen persuades Longshanks's Irish soldiers to change sides, and at first it looks as if Wallace might win. But the Scottish nobles betray Wallace, and one – Robert the Bruce – actually fights for Longshanks. Wallace is defeated and badly wounded. But Bruce is so ashamed of himself that he promises to fight for Scotland from now on.

Wallace kills the nobles who betrayed him, and wages guerrilla war against the English. Longshanks tries to trick Wallace again using Isabelle, but Wallace avoids capture. He meets with Isabelle for a second time, and they fall in love, and she becomes pregnant with his baby.

In the end, however, Wallace is betrayed when he goes to meet Robert the Bruce. He is put on trial, sentenced to death, and horribly executed. As he dies, he shouts: 'Freedom!' At the same time, Longshanks dies too – but Isabelle tortures his dying moments by telling him that the baby she carries is not his grandson, but Wallace's child.

The story does not end with Wallace's death, but with the Battle of Bannockburn, 1314, as Robert the Bruce and an army of Scottish patriots, inspired by Wallace's example, charge the English army and throw them out of Scotland forever.

Activities

1. Study the story of *Braveheart*. Remember that most of it is fictional. Make a list of the NINE main events of the story.
2. Imagine you are William Wallace. Tell the story from your 'own' point of view.
3. Now tell the story from the point of view of other people – Edward I, a Scottish warrior, Isabelle of France, Stephen the Irish fighter … and finally, yourself.

Knowledge: The truth about Braveheart

You cannot ignore the historical errors in *Braveheart*. Here are some of the howlers – though you will find out about many more as you read this book:

Edward was not a pagan (he went on Crusade), he did not hurt any of his son's gay lovers, and he **NEVER** murdered any nobles in any barns.

Edward I did not invite the Norman lords to Scotland, and he certainly did not give them the right of *primae noctis*, which never existed in England or Scotland.

Scots did not wear kilts until 1600. Having Wallace's Scots wear kilts is like making a film of Oliver Cromwell in which he wears jeans.

William Wallace may have been born near Glasgow, or near Ayr, but he certainly did **NOT** live in the Highlands. Wallace was a knight. He was never a crofter, and would not have dressed like one.

Edward invaded Scotland in 1296, not 1280. In fact, in 1280 Scotland was happily ruled by Alexander III and England was at peace with Scotland.

The Scots won the Battle of Stirling Bridge because they attacked the English army while it was crossing Stirling Bridge. *Braveheart* did not show a bridge because 'it got in the way' of the action. Wallace did not invent 'long spears' as a way to stop cavalry.

Robert the Bruce did not fight for Edward at Falkirk, although he joined Edward I in 1302. And he did not need **Wallace** to convince him that he wanted to be king. His father had claimed the crown before him, and Robert changed sides, abandoned his family and murdered his rivals to become king, finally grabbing the throne in 1306.

'Murron' never existed. 'Marion Braidfute' was added into the story of *The Wallace* in the sixteenth century by the Braidfute family, who wanted to trace back their family to **Wallace**. Her 'marriage' to **Wallace** was added in the nineteenth century. And her name was changed to Murron for *Braveheart*, so people did not confuse her with Maid Marion in the stories of Robin Hood.

In 1298, when the film has Edward sending Isabelle to talk with **Wallace**, she was in reality only three years old. She did not come to England and marry Edward II until 1308, a year after Edward I died, and three years after **Wallace** died. Edward III – supposedly the son of **Wallace** and Isabelle – was not born until 1312.

Braveheart gets the military facts of William **Wallace** all wrong. **Wallace** never captured York, and it was not Edward's Irish soldiers who refused to fight at Falkirk, but the Welsh.

Edward I did not die at the same time as **Wallace** in 1305, but two years later, in 1307.

Activities

In 1996, *Braveheart* won five Oscars – best film, best director, best sound effects, best make-up and best camera-work (especially for the Battle of Stirling scene). Write an article for your local newspaper saying whether you think it deserves this. You may want to:

- Describe the story of the film.
- Say whether you found the film exciting or boring and why.
- Comment on how historically accurate the film is (using the information on pages 8–9).

Interpretations: Does it matter?

This is what one historian has written about the film *Braveheart*:

'*Enjoy the film as a fantasy film, by all means – just as one enjoys* Star Wars – *simply do not mistake it for history. The events aren't accurate, the dates aren't accurate, the characters aren't accurate, the names aren't accurate, the clothes aren't accurate – in short, just about nothing is accurate.*'

Sharon L Krossa, *Regarding the Film Braveheart* (2001)
Krossa has a PhD in History from the University of Aberdeen.

But if (as pupils are taught nowadays) history is just a matter of **interpretation**, why can't *Braveheart* re-interpret history however it wants and still be just as valid? These sources will help you consider whether it matters if those nitpicking historians tell you Braveheart got the facts wrong.

SOURCE 1

As the film begins, a voice-over is heard saying this:

I shall tell you of William Wallace. Historians from England will say I am a liar, but history is written by those who have hanged heroes.

Script of *Braveheart* (1995)

SOURCE 2

Braveheart achieved all of its historical objectives. Hoping for realism, it gave a believable interpretation that let the audience sympathise with William Wallace, get to know the period, and get a basic understanding of the events … The *feel* and the underlying *truth* of the film was shown. The general accuracy of the film was spot on – even if the specific details weren't.

From an internet blog (2007)

SOURCE 3

People have invested his times with battles that are being fought now, and with meanings that were not appropriate for the time.

A wargamer writing on a web forum (2006)

SOURCE 4

Pointing out *Braveheart's* numerous historical errors is mostly irrelevant … Its purpose is to inspire rather than to instruct. Whilst the film's history may be bunk, it reveals a deeper truth, the truth that nations live on myth, and, anyway, myth is usually more exciting than reality. This film shows the way it ought to have happened.

From a film review on the internet (1995)

SOURCE 5

Actor Mel Gibson flirts with actress Catherine McCormack in the film *Braveheart* (1995). Does it matter that 'Murron' never existed, and that the courting, wedding and relationship shown in the film – while it might be true for modern couples – is totally wrong for the thirteenth century?

SOURCE 6

One of Mel Gibson's 'trademarks' as an actor is his very meaningful use of his eyes. Does it matter that he used exactly the same eye-movements playing a thirteenth-century outlaw in *Braveheart* (1995, shown right) as he did for a twentieth-century gangster in the film *Payback* (1999, shown far right)?

SOURCE 7

This caricature of a Scotsman comes from *This is Scotland*, written by the Scottish photographer David Webster in 1964.

'Ceud mile failte agus slainte mhor' on the mat is Scottish Gaelic and means: 'A hundred thousand welcomes and great health'.

Webster described Scotland as 'a wild and rugged country of mountains and moors, entirely inhabited by kilted, caber-tossing, porridge- and haggis-eating Highlanders'.

SOURCE 8

This caricature of a Scotsman comes from the film, *Braveheart* (1995), made by an Australian actor. It portrayed Scotland as a wild and rugged country, inhabited by kilted, violent, unwashed, fearless Highlanders.

Activities

1. Is Sharon Krossa being nasty about *Braveheart*? Explain what she is saying in your own words.
2. Discuss Sources 1–4, trying to understand what they are saying. Which is the odd one out? Why?
3. What does the writer of Source 3 mean? Explain and develop his ideas in your own words.
4. Sources 5 and 6 are about 'anachronism' – about putting modern things like modern eye-movements and relationships into a story about the past. Does this matter, or does it just help modern audiences understand? Would it have spoiled the film if Wallace had shot the English with a machine-gun?
5. Do you consider Source 7 to be an insulting racist caricature? If you do, what do you think about Source 8?

Knowledge: Invaders of Scotland

Where do you think the Scots came from?

Fifty years ago, schoolchildren were taught that the history of the British Isles consisted of 'waves of invaders' – Celts, Saxons, Vikings, Normans – who had come through the centuries to steal and to settle. They were taught – what seemed at the time an amusing puzzle – that the Scots came from Ireland, the Welsh came from England, and the English came from Germany.

Armed with the latest DNA tests, historians are now able to say that, in fact, the people of Great Britain are overwhelmingly from … Spain! Our most common gene group, R1b, comes from an ancient people in northern Spain who survived the Ice Age, and moved northwards into the British Isles after c.10,000 BC.

None of the 'invaders' who came after them came in big enough numbers to affect the basic gene pool. The Angles seem to have affected south-east England, and there is Viking blood in the Orkney Islands. But if you fancied that the Scots are 'a race apart', you are going to be disappointed. The English are 64 per cent R1b, the Scots 75 per cent, and the Welsh and the Irish 90 per cent+.

Our ancestors may have originally come from Spain, but that is not to say that we have not been affected by the 'invaders' who have come since! Each of the invaders who have driven northwards into Scotland have made their mark upon the land and the people.

The Romans

When the Romans invaded in AD 43, they found Celtic-speaking tribes whom we call 'the Britons'.

Although they conquered England, the Romans were unable to subdue Scotland (though they won the battle of Mons Graupius in AD 84).

The Romans tried a number of 'frontiers' as the northern limit of their empire (see map, left).

The tribes in England and the Lowlands of Scotland, became 'Romanised'. The Highland tribes (whom the Romans started to call the 'Picts') constantly attacked Roman lands.

The Anglo-Saxons

In AD 407 the Roman armies left Britain, and the British tribes were left undefended.

Invaders (called the 'Scots') crossed over from Ireland, and established the kingdom of Dál Riata in what we now call Argyll.

The Anglo-Saxons who invaded England also expanded steadily into the Lowlands. They even invaded the Highlands, but were turned back at the battle of Nechtansmere in AD 685.

The map on the right shows the post-Roman kingdoms in Scotland. The blue line shows Dál Riata at its greatest extent (c. AD 600), and the green line shows the Anglo-Saxon kingdom of Bernicia c. AD 800.

We know from DNA testing that the Anglo-Saxons did not *replace* the British tribes; they came as conquerors – taking over only the land and the government.

And how much difference did they make to Scotland? Certainly none in the Highlands, because they never conquered there, but maybe more in the Lowlands, where they ruled for perhaps 300 years.

The map on the right shows places in England and Scotland that have Anglo-Saxon place-names. It shows how limited Anglo-Saxon influence was, even in the Lowlands.

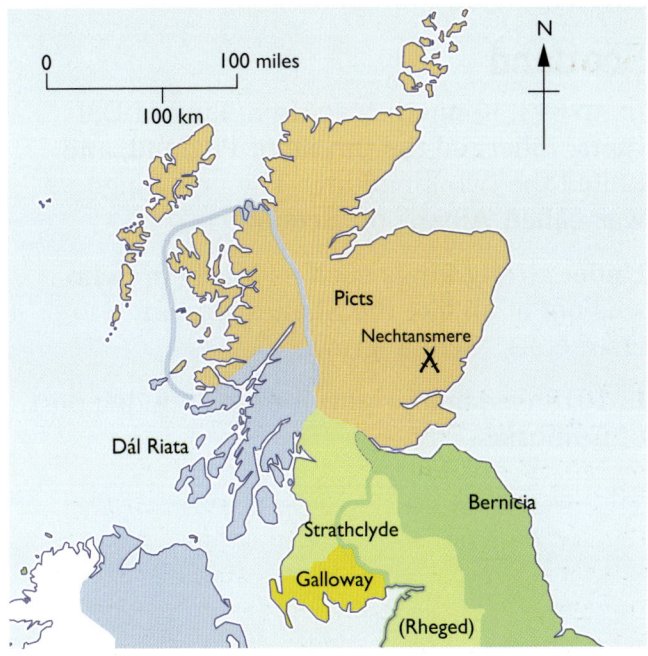

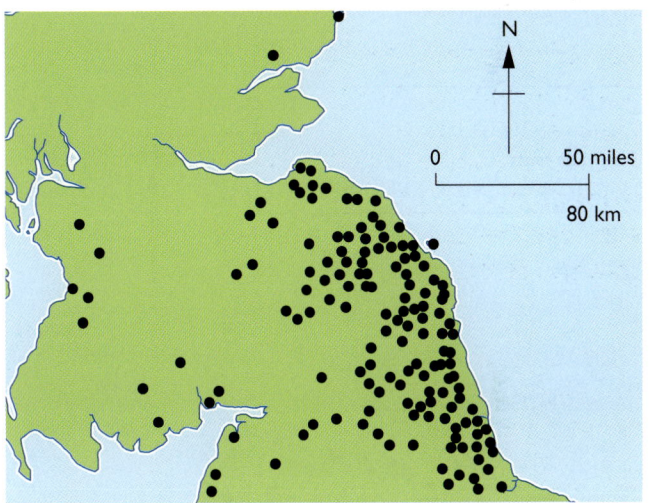

The Vikings

After AD 800 came another wave of invaders – the Vikings, from Denmark and Norway.

The Vikings had a huge impact in Orkney and Shetland, but again the evidence both of DNA and of place-names (see map, left) suggests that, although they became the rulers of large areas, they did not make very much difference to the ordinary (Gaelic) people elsewhere in Scotland.

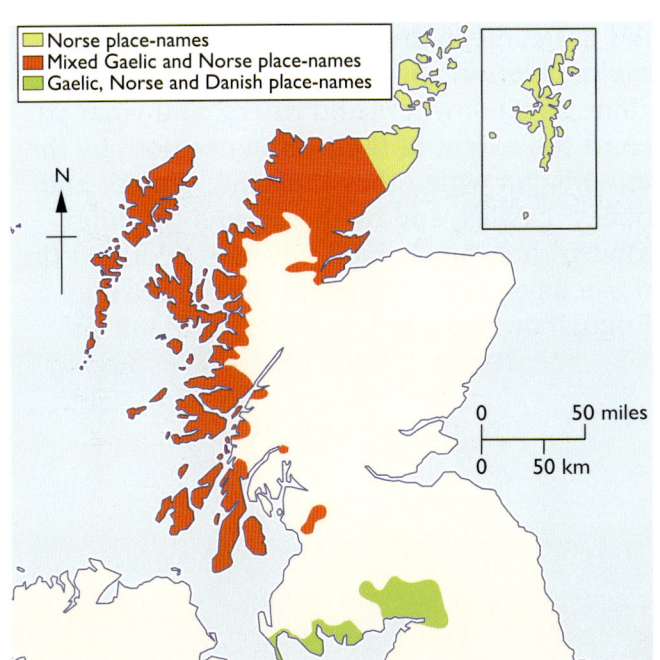

Norse place-names
Mixed Gaelic and Norse place-names
Gaelic, Norse and Danish place-names

Scotland

In AD 843, Kenneth MacAlpin, king of Dál Riata, inherited the throne of Pictland, and united the two kingdoms. The new kingdom was called 'Alban', or 'Scotia'.

Under strong kings such as Macbeth (who was not at all like the Shakespearian character), 'Scotia' grew.

In 1018 (see map, right) it even included part of Cumbria.

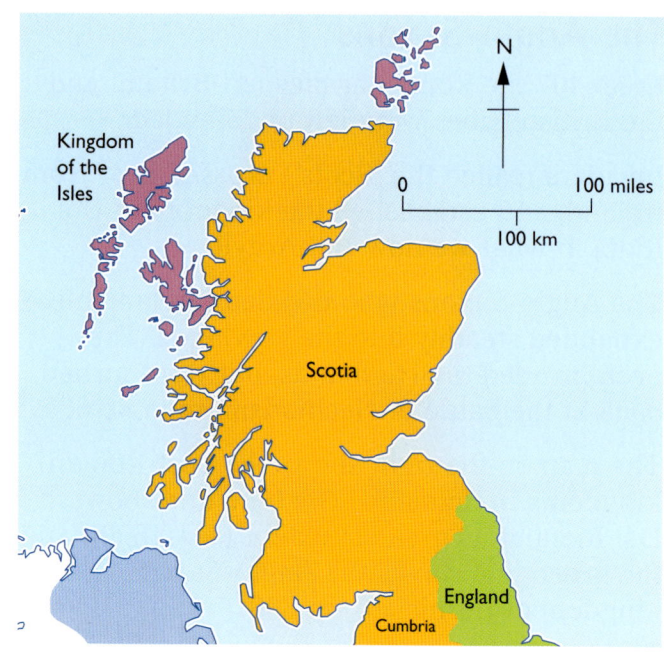

The Normans

The final invasion was that of the Normans.

William of Normandy conquered England in 1066, and invaded Scotland in 1072, forcing Malcolm II of Scotland to do homage to him.

Gradually the Normans moved north into Scotland. The Scottish king David I (1124–53) had been brought up in England and he actually invited the Normans to come to Scotland; this was invasion by invitation.

Like the 'invaders' before them, the Normans did not come in great numbers to drive out the population and resettle the land. They came as landowners and rulers, and you can chart the extent of their influence both by the mounds on which they built their 'motte and bailey' castles, and by the burghs (trading towns) that they helped set up in Scotland (in those days, most traders in Scotland were English or Flemings).

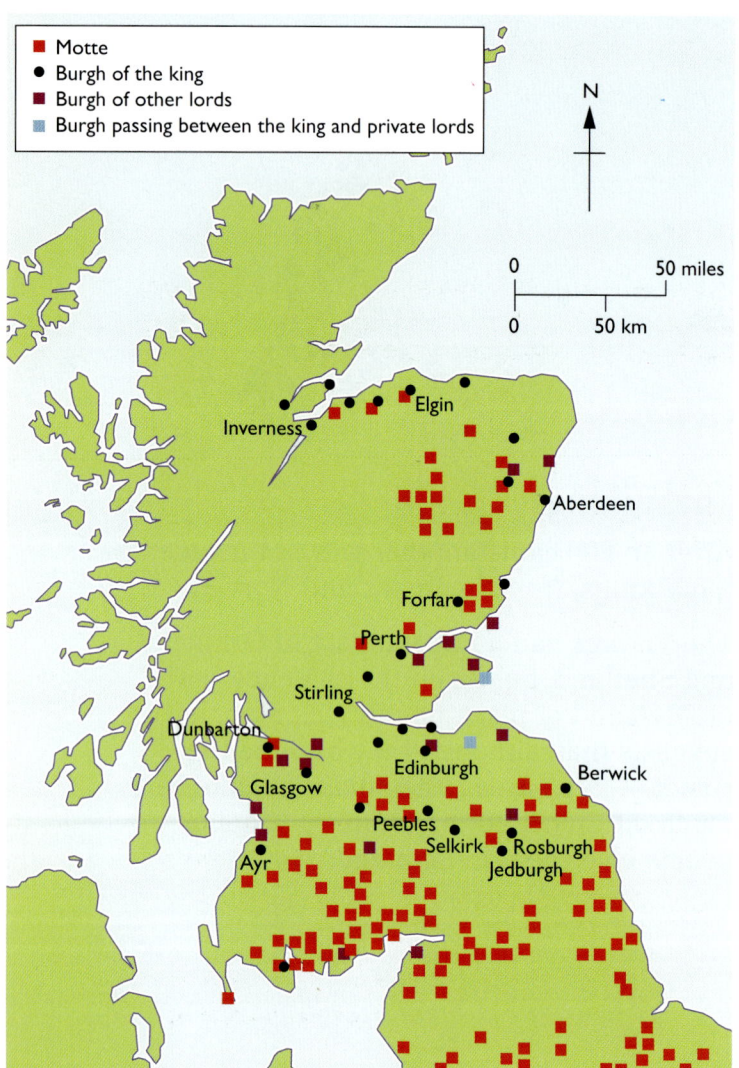

The Normans took their ideas of 'feudalism', 'knights', chivalry and trade to Scotland. But perhaps the most important change that these Norman settlers caused was that, after about AD 1200, 'Gaelic' (the language of the 'Scots') began to be replaced by 'Scots' – a dialect of Anglo-Saxon English.

Here is an example:

> ‘*Our ald ennemys cummyn of Saxonys blud*
> *That nevyr yeit to Scotland wald do gud*
> *It is weyle knawyne on mony divers syde*
> *How thai haff wrocht in to thar mychty pryde*
> *To hald Scotlande at undyr evermar,*
> *Bot God abuff has maid thar mycht to par*
> *And hensfurth I will my proces hald*
> *Of Wilyham Wallas yhe haf hard beyne tald* ’

Blind Harry, *The Wallace* (c. 1475)

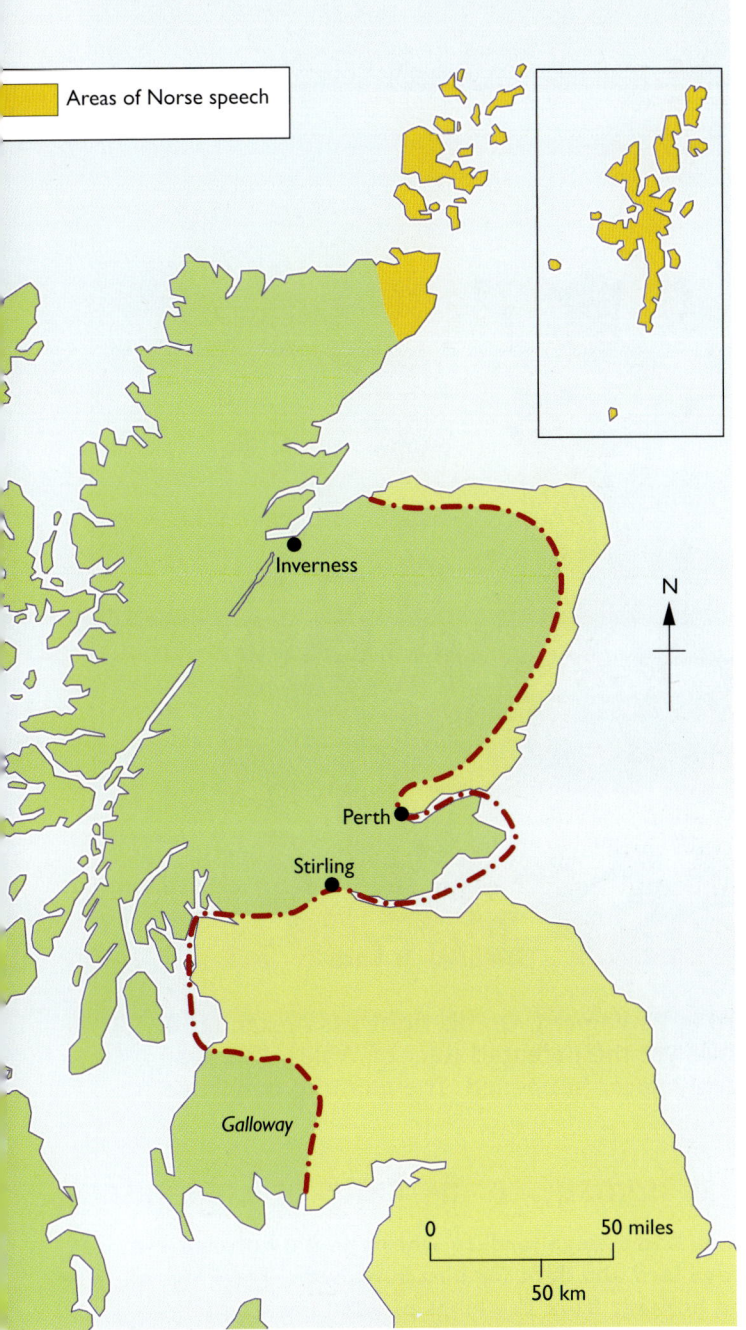

Areas of Norse speech

Inverness

Perth

Stirling

Galloway

N

0   50 miles

50 km

The map shows the areas of Scotland which still spoke Gaelic in 1400. South and east of the line, the Scots spoke Scots-English. So the map shows the areas of Scotland which had been most 'Normanised' by 1400. The map is interesting because it suggests that in 1300 there were THREE 'Scotlands' – a Norse Orkney in the far north; the Highlands (which had been undefeated and unchanged by any of the invaders); and the Lowlands, which had been conquered, changed and modernised time after time by foreign invaders coming north from England.

Activities

1. Romans – Anglo-Saxons – Vikings – Normans. Use pages 12–15 to make brief notes on each of these 'invasions' of Scotland. Which one made the most difference to Scotland, would you say?
2. When, in your opinion, is it first possible to start meaningfully calling Scotland: 'Scotland'?
3. Yes or No: Were the Normans welcome when they came to Scotland? Explain your answer.

4. Read the extract from Blind Harry on this page. You will find it easier to understand if you read it out loud – just read it phonetically, as it looks. Do the best job you can to write it out in modern language.
5. During William Wallace's wars, most of his support came from Galloway and the Highlands. Use the information on pages 12–15 to come up with a theory (or theories) why.

CHAPTER 3

Crisis in Scotland

Knowledge: A disputed succession

Alexander III became king of Scotland in 1249. He was a good king, and his reign has been called the 'golden age' of Scottish history. It was a time of peace and prosperity, and Scotland grew more powerful – in 1266 Alexander conquered the Hebrides and the Isle of Man from Norway.

The only problem was who would be the next king. Alexander married Princess Margaret of England, but she died in 1275 and all three of their children died before 1283.

Alexander remarried a French princess (Yolande) with whom he genuinely seems to have fallen in love – but rushing home to his young wife one dark night in 1286 he fell from his horse and was killed.

When Yolande's unborn child was stillborn, Scotland was left without a ruler.

A painting showing Edward in Parliament. On his right sits Alexander III of Scotland, on his left Llewellyn, the defeated ruler of Wales. This is an imaginary scene that probably never happened. The painting may have been done in 1524.

Did Scottish kings pay homage to the kings of England?

In the feudal system, everyone had a 'liege lord' to whom he did homage. He was expected to obey his liege lord and fight for him in his wars. The kings of England had long demanded homage from the kings of Scotland – and sometimes they got it.

- Malcolm III gave homage to William the Conqueror in 1072.
- Malcolm IV did homage to Henry II of England for his possessions in Henry's kingdom in 1157 and 1163.
- William I did homage to Richard I for 14 years (1174–89), and to King John in 1200.

However, it was always uncertain whether the kings of Scotland were doing homage for the kingdom of Scotland, or just for the lands they owned in England.

Alexander refused to pay homage to England, and in 1278, when Edward I forced the issue, Alexander specifically excluded Scotland – 'No one has a right to homage for my kingdom save God alone, and I hold it only of God'.

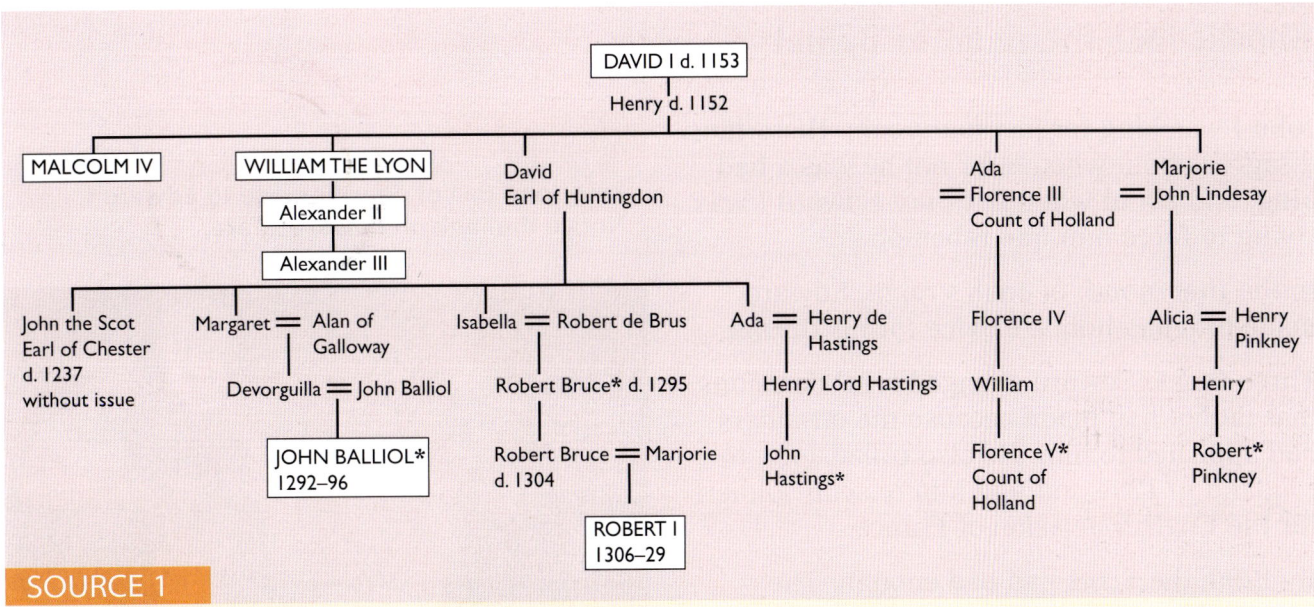

SOURCE 1

The disputed succession. Claimants are marked with an asterisk*. Kings are in capitals in boxes.

Next in line to the throne of Scotland was the daughter of King Erik of Norway, 'Margaret, the Maid of Norway'. Edward I hoped that she would marry his son Edward (which would have united England and Scotland peacefully), but Margaret ruined his plans by dying of seasickness on the way to Scotland in 1290.

SOURCE 2

Seeing that we claim to have right to the kingdom of Scotland; and Edward, King of England, has shown to us, by good and sufficient reasons, that to him belongs the sovereign lordship of the said kingdom of Scotland, and the right of hearing and deciding our case. We, of our own will, without any force or pressure, agree to receive justice before him as sovereign lord of the land.

Letter of the claimants to Edward I (5 June 1291). This promise is known as 'the Declaration of Norham'.

By now there were THIRTEEN claimants to the throne of Scotland. Faced by the likelihood of a long civil war, the leading nobles of Scotland (called the 'Guardians') came to Edward I and asked him to decide who should be king. (Some historians have called this 'The Great Cause'.)

First, however, Edward demanded that all thirteen claimants promise they would do homage to him if he chose them as the next king.

The Scots were not happy about this, but what else could they do? In June 1291, they agreed.

The process dragged on, and it was not until November 1292 that Edward's judges ruled in favour of John Balliol, a great-great-great-grandson of King David I.

Activities

1. Explain what 'doing homage' was.
2. Why was it important for the people of Scotland that Scotland's kings only did homage for their lands in England?
3. Why, do you think, did all thirteen claimants promise to do homage to Edward if they won?
4. Imagine you are John Balliol. Using Source 1, explain your claim to the throne in words.
5. Who would YOU have chosen, if you were Edward I?

Knowledge: The reign of Balliol

John I was king for just four years. Historians disagree about whether or not he was a bad king, and about whether or not Edward I was trying to force him into rebellion.

In the first month of John's reign, Edward made him pay homage twice for his throne.

Three times, Edward changed legal decisions that Balliol had made because the offenders had appealed to him. He also called John to England in 1294 and told him to send soldiers for the English invasion of France.

By 1295, the Scots had had enough. The Guardians met in Stirling in July 1295. With – or without (historians disagree) – John's agreement, they refused to send soldiers, and instead made an alliance with the king of France.

Both sides prepared for war, but it was the Scots who attacked first. In 1296 they attacked Northumberland, and then they invaded Cumbria and ransacked the villages around Carlisle.

King John Balliol does homage to Edward I. Notice the look on Edward's face.

The MacDuff Case

- MacDuff, brother of the Earl of Fife, claimed that he owned some land in Fife.
- MacDuff behaved badly and Balliol put him in prison.
- MacDuff appealed to Edward I.
- Edward called Balliol to Parliament in November 1293, and asked him to explain what he had done.
- Balliol said that it was a matter for the Scottish Parliament. He did not want to be treated as one of Edward's nobles.
- King Edward was angry, and forced Balliol to admit that he had done homage for the kingdom of Scotland.
- Instead, Balliol now asked for time to seek advice from the Scottish Parliament, and was given until May 1295.
- Once back in Scotland, Balliol ignored Edward.

Activities

1. Look at Source 1 (above). Describe what is happening in your own words. Now look at the expressions on the faces of the people, and their body language. What are they *thinking*?
2. What do you think? Was Edward just requiring from Balliol what he had been promised at Norham – or was he trying to drive Balliol into rebellion? Use the facts on pages 18–19 in your answer.
3. Why do you think Balliol was nicknamed 'Toom Tabard'?
4. Look at Source 2 (opposite). The artist has made it look rather like queuing up for a lottery ticket. Is there anything good about this representation? Would you have interpreted it differently? How would you have represented the surroundings? Edward I? The English? The Scottish nobles?

Immediately, Edward invaded Scotland. On 30 March he captured Berwick, and on 27 April the English army beat the Scots at the battle of Dunbar. After that, Edward marched unopposed to Edinburgh, and on to Stirling, and then northwards as far as Inverness.

On 7 July Balliol surrendered, and three days later he went to the Bishop of Durham at Brechin, where his royal coat of arms was torn from his clothes. Thereafter he was called 'Toom Tabard' ('empty coat').

Edward imprisoned Balliol and his son in the Tower. With him to London went the Stone of Destiny, on which the kings of Scotland were crowned, along with all the Scottish government's legal documents.

Finally, returning to Berwick in October, Edward asked 2,000 of Scotland's leading men to do homage to him, in writing, signing what came to be called the 'Ragman Rolls' (after all the bits of ribbon hanging from the seals).

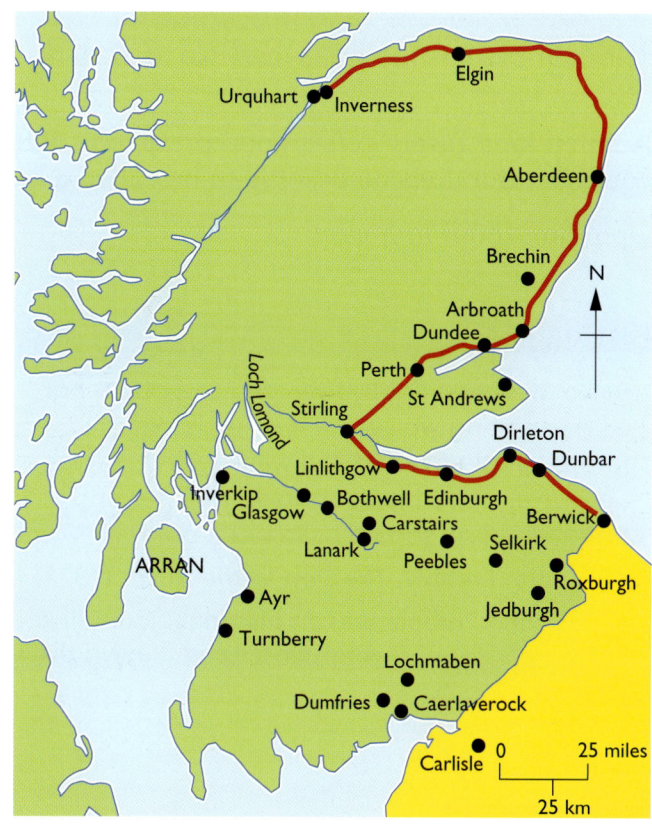

Edward I's invasion, 1296

SOURCE 2

An artist's reconstruction of Scottish landowners signing the Ragman Rolls.

Interpretations: Was Balliol a bad king?

A failed king rarely gets a good press, and John Balliol's reputation is just about as bad as it could be. But does he deserve to be called a bad king?

Opinions about him vary:

SOURCE 1

Balliol has been rightly regarded as a puppet or a lamb among wolves. He was in his early forties, simple-minded and weak-willed. He was never well, foolishly haughty in manner, and timid when he should have been bold.

John Prebble, *The Lion in the North* (1971)

John Prebble was an historian, journalist, scriptwriter and playwright.

SOURCE 2

Balliol was a known weakling; an ordinary man put into an impossible position. His conduct may have been due to ill-health, domestic difficulty, and a haughty mind; but it may also be interpreted as a deliberate attempt by Edward to drive Balliol to his destruction.

JD Mackie, *A History of Scotland* (1964)

John Mackie was Professor of History at the University of Glasgow.

SOURCE 3

Balliol was a puppet king put in place by Edward I, an English king. Do not dare to put Balliol on this page. The only decent thing Balliol did was move to France and die.

Comment on a Scottish internet blog (2007)

SOURCE 4

Little is known of the reign of King John. To call it the reign of 'Toom Tabard' is a stark example of reading history backwards. The nickname was not applied by John's subjects during his reign, but later, after the ritual humiliation inflicted when he was stripped of his tabard and knightly girdle.

Michael Lynch, *Scotland: A New History* (1991)

Michael Lynch was Senior Lecturer in History at the University of Edinburgh.

SOURCE 5

Balliol's reputation resulted from the propaganda of the man who stole his throne, Robert Bruce, and the pro-Bruce writers who followed him. The reality of Balliol's reign is rather more successful than will fit the 'weak and incompetent' stamp that is usually placed upon it.

Fiona Watson, *Under the Hammer* (1998)

Fiona Watson is Lecturer in History at the University of Stirling.

SOURCE 6

He made a worthwhile effort at government. We must look beyond the powerful legend of Balliol the feeble puppet, laughed off the throne by scornful Scots. It is true he was not a forceful man and certainly no match for Edward I. But he was not a nonentity.

GWS Barrow, *Robert Bruce* (2005)

GWS Barrow is professor emeritus at the University of Edinburgh, and a respected expert on medieval history.

This artwork for a book on 'Scottish Heroes' shows Rob Roy, Robert the Bruce, William Wallace, Mary Queen of Scots and Robert Burns – King John Balliol is noticeable only by his absence.

The reign of Balliol – the facts

- He did homage to Edward for the kingdom of Scotland.
- When he started to rule, almost half the nobles did not support him, and there were twelve disappointed rivals. By 1296 almost all the Scottish nobles supported him.
- He had – and kept – the support of the powerful Comyn family.
- He held four Parliaments 1293–94.
- He took back crown lands lost since the death of Alexander III in 1286.
- He held courts to put right all the wrongs done since 1286.
- He appointed sheriffs to the Kingdom of the Isles to try to increase royal power there.
- Twice (1292 and 1293) he allowed Edward to overturn legal decisions he had made.
- In 1294 he refused to obey Edward's order to change his decision to imprison MacDuff, and he refused to go to London again when called.
- In 1295 twelve Guardians met and agreed with Balliol to refuse to send soldiers to Edward's army.
- In 1295 he sent four nobles to make an alliance and marriage treaty with France – the start of the 'auld alliance'.
- William Wallace and the Scottish nobility fought for eight years for King John, even though he was held a prisoner by Edward I.

Activities

1. Look at Sources 1–6.
   a) Which ones suggest that Balliol was a bad king?
   b) Study them, and make a list of the points they make against him.
   c) Find a fact on pages 18–21 that supports each point.
2. Look again at Sources 1–6.
   a) Which ones suggest that Balliol was *not* a bad king?
   b) Study them, and make a list of the points they make for him.
3. Look at the provenances of Sources 1–6. Which strike you as being most reliable? Why?
4. Look at the 'facts' of Balliol's reign (above). Choose your 'Top Three Things Balliol Did', and explain why they make him look a good king.
5. What do YOU think about Balliol? Express your opinion and find some facts that prove it.

Using evidence: The sack of Berwick, 1296

At Berwick, the English army slaughtered the townspeople. One English chronicler, Matthew of Westminster, put the number of dead at 60,000 – three times the population of the whole town at that time! Another Englishman – Walter of Hemingburgh – put the number at about 7,000. The Scottish historian James MacKay estimates the slain at up to 20,000, and calls it 'the worst atrocity ever to stain the pages of English history'.

Why did Edward do this? Maybe he was angry at the taunts the defenders had shouted when he called on them to surrender (by the rules of war at that time, if a garrison refused to surrender, the attackers were entitled to kill everyone in the town). Or just before the attack, Edward's cousin, Richard of Cornwall, had been killed by a chance arrow, so maybe he wanted revenge. MacKay suggests Edward did it as an example – that he wanted to 'terrorise and cow' the Scots. Mel Gibson simply calls Edward 'a psychopath'.

This is how one Scottish chronicler, Andrew of Wyntoun, describes the event:

SOURCE 1

And when the gates opened then
Fast rushed in the English men,
And surrounded the Scottish there
For they knew well what they were
The English there slew down
All the Scottish nation
Both old and young, men and wives,
And suckling children, they took their lives.
Thus they slaughtered so fast
All the day, until at last
King Edward saw, at that time,
A woman slain, and from her side
A baby he saw fall out, sprawling
Beside that slain woman, laying.
'*Laissez, laissez,*' then cried he;
'Leave off, leave off,' is what that means.

Seven thousand and five hundred were
The bodies reckoned, that were slain there;
This was done on the Good Friday.
Of age, nor kind – none spared they.
Two days on, as a deep flood,
Through all the town there ran red blood.
Thus that King of England,
(Not king, but a foul tyrant,)
Led that day his devotions
He made them suffer their Passion.

Andrew of Wyntoun, *The Origynale Cronykil of Scotland* (1420)

The attack did not take place on Good Friday, as Wyntoun claimed. It took place on 30 March – a week later. Edward waited on purpose until Easter was over.

English chroniclers agree that there was great slaughter, but say that Edward let the women and children leave first.

Activities

1. Find four different possible reasons why Edward allowed the atrocity at Berwick. For each, explain WHY it might have led Edward to allow the slaughter.
2. Compare Source 1 with Source 2. How does the drawing support the poem? How does it contradict the poem?
3. Look at the list of atrocities in modern history (right).
   a) What makes an atrocity – is it just a matter of numbers?
   b) Compared to these modern atrocities, how badly does the sack of Berwick rate?

Some famous atrocities in modern history

1905 **Bloody Sunday**, Russia: the Tsar set his soldiers on a peaceful demonstration – perhaps 1000 dead.

1919 **Amritsar**, India: the British army under General Dyer fired on an unarmed crowd – official number of dead, 349.

1937 **Nanking**, China: perhaps 40,000 Chinese inhabitants slaughtered over six weeks by the Japanese Army.

1944 **Oradour-sur-Glane**, France: the SS killed 245 women, 207 children and 196 men in revenge for French Resistance attacks.

1968 **My Lai**, Vietnam: American soldiers killed more than 400 peaceful villagers.

1995 **Srebrenica**, Bosnia: pro-Serb militiamen massacred 8,373 Bosniaks.

2001 **September 11**, New York, USA: Al Qaeda attacked the World Trade Center, killing 2,793.

SOURCE 2

A drawing of the sack of Berwick, done about 30 years after the event.

CHAPTER 4

William Wallace

Knowledge: Wallace's Rebellion

Having got rid of Balliol, Edward left Scotland in October 1296, commenting that: 'a man who gets rid of a shit does a good job'. He put the Earl of Warenne (his army commander) in charge of Scotland, with Hugh Cressingham as Treasurer.

But if Edward thought he had conquered Scotland, he was wrong. The first hint of trouble came from Cressingham: the Scots were refusing to pay their taxes.

> *From the time you left not a penny could be raised from the Scots, unless my lord Warenne shall enter your land and make them pay.*

Letter from Hugh Cressingham to Edward I, July 1297

Shortly afterwards, reports came of English sheriffs who did not dare to go to their Scottish lands because it was too dangerous.

At this point, in May 1297, in the words of the Scottish chronicler John of Fordun: 'William Wallace lifted up his head'. Wallace's murder of William Hazelrig, the English sheriff of Lanark, is traditionally taken as the starting point of the rebellion, though the truth of the matter is that it was actually started by Andrew Moray in the far north of Scotland. Even in Lanark – if Wallace did start an uprising – it is possible that he was put up to it by Bishop Wishart of Glasgow and a noble called James the Steward (Wallace's lord).

Wallace, however, was a figurehead, and became an inspiration to the Scots. First, Moray and Wallace won the battle of Stirling Bridge on 11 September 1297. Then they invaded England. They did not capture York, as the film *Braveheart* suggests, but they did terrify the people of northern Britain – a tactic Scottish kings were to use again in the future.

SOURCE 1

Andrew Moray and William Wallace, leaders of the Scotch army and the community of the same kingdom, send to the people of Lübeck and Hamburg, greetings.

We have been told that you have been helpful and friendly to us and our merchants. We ask you to tell your merchants that they can now come safely to Scotland, because the Kingdom of Scotland has, thanks be to God, by war been recovered from the power of the English.

Farewell. Given on the 11th day of October in the Year of Grace 1297.

We also pray you to be good to John Burnet and John Frere, our merchants, just as you might wish that we should help your merchants. Farewell.

A letter of Moray and Wallace to merchants in Germany. It is the only surviving document written by Wallace.

The nobles made Wallace 'Guardian' (military leader), although he never ruled Scotland – the nobles did that in the name of King John Balliol. And Wallace did his job. If any Scots helped the English, Wallace burned their crops and their houses. If they would not join the Scots army, Wallace hanged them. And when the English invaded, Wallace burned everything in the enemy's path.

But Moray died in November 1297, and on 22 July 1298 Wallace was defeated at the battle of Falkirk. He resigned as Guardian, and in August 1299 he left for France without telling anybody. According to Blind Harry, Wallace went to France to get help. Other writers suggest he was in a deep depression.

Wallace stayed abroad until 1303. On his return, he fought the battle of Rosslyn (which the Scots won) on 23 February. Afterwards, he led guerrilla raids on the English, but he did not have much success. Rather, he seems to have spent most of the time on the run from the English.

SOURCE 2

Historians know next to nothing about Wallace, and most of the stories about him are legend rather than fact. One of the stories about Wallace, told by the English chronicler Walter of Hemingburgh, is that when he was raiding England in the winter of 1297 he found two monks at Hexham trying to take communion; he stopped his men robbing them, and gave them his protection.

This drawing, from an old children's history book, is an artist's reconstruction of this legend.

SOURCE 3

We, Andrew Moray and William Wallace, the leaders of the army of the realm of Scotland, in the name of John, king of Scotland, with the agreement of the community of the kingdom, greeting.

We inform you that we have taken into the peace of the king and ourselves the prior and convent of Hexham in Northumberland. Therefore we strictly forbid anyone to inflict on them any injury or hurt, in pain of loss of life and limb.

Hexham, 7 November 1297

The original of this letter, if it ever existed, has been lost – it exists only as copies made by Walter of Hemingburgh.

Activities

What can a historian learn from Source 1 about:
1. a) Wallace?
   b) the war?
2. Compare Source 2 with Source 3. How does the letter support the drawing?
3. Imagine you are a Scottish newspaper editor. Write headlines for the front page articles on the following dates:
   a) October 1296
   b) May 1297
   c) 11 September 1297
   d) 22 July 1298
   e) August 1299
   f) 23 February 1303
   For each date, write a brief note to your journalist telling them what you want the article to be about.

Interpretations: Was Wallace a great general?

The Battle of Stirling Bridge, 11 September 1297

The Battle according to *Braveheart*

William Wallace invents the idea of long spears to defeat the English heavy cavalry. He arrives with them just as the Highlanders – alarmed by the huge numbers of English soldiers – are about to desert. He inspires them with a brilliant speech about freedom, and teaches them in seconds how to use the spears.

The battle is a pitched, arranged medieval battle on a flat field. Wallace goes to pick a fight with the English commander, briefing the nobles on the way back about how he wants to use their cavalry. The Scots moon the English, and use the spears to stop the English cavalry. Then they charge and the Scottish cavalry outflank and rout the English, who are slaughtered.

What actually happened

Warenne, the English Commander, turned up late; he hated Scotland's wet weather, and had slept in. Cressingham, the English treasurer, wanted to get on with the battle. He asked permission to take the troops across the river to the battlefield.

A narrow bridge was the only way across the river. On top of a nearby hill the Scots – greatly outnumbered by the English – waited. Andrew Moray, the leader of the successful northern rebellion, had been joined by William Wallace.

When the first half of the English army had crossed the river, the Scots rushed down the valley-side and attacked them.

The English army was still crossing the bridge and not ready. The Scots trapped them and drove them back into the river, where the weight of their armour drowned them. About the same time the bridge collapsed, either because English engineers pulled it down to cover their retreat, or because of the chaos of English cavalry trying to turn around and get away. Warenne and the rest of the English army fled.

The English were slaughtered. It was claimed that Wallace had Cressingham skinned, and used his skin, perhaps as a sword-belt.

The Battle of Falkirk, 22 July 1298

The Battle according to *Braveheart*

Tricked by Edward, Wallace rushes back to Scotland to meet an English invasion. He persuades the nobles to fight. The night before the battle, his men pour oil onto the battlefield.

At first the battle goes well for Wallace. Irish Stephen persuades Edward's Irish fighters to join the Scots. Then Wallace sets fire to the oil, which causes chaos in the English cavalry. But when he signals the nobles to attack with their cavalry, they betray him and ride away.

The Scots are slaughtered and Wallace is wounded.

What actually happened

As Edward advanced into Scotland in 1298, Wallace burned the fields before him. Edward's soldiers were starving. His Welshmen, after a drunken riot, ended up in a brawl with the English soldiers and were refusing to fight. He was about to go home when he got news that Wallace was nearby.

Wallace could have retreated, but he chose to fight, perhaps because he knew that Edward's army was in such poor shape. He drew up his army at the top of a hill, behind a bog and a stream. He formed his men into packs called schiltrons, their long spears pointing outwards. When the English cavalry attacked, they were slowed down by the bog, and could not break through the schiltrons. So Edward used his archers to break up the schiltrons, and the cavalry finished off the job.

The Scottish cavalry did withdraw, and the pro-Bruce chroniclers did accuse their leader, Red Comyn, of betraying Wallace. But Comyn led the Scottish army for the next six years and lost everything fighting the English – it is perhaps more likely that, seeing the battle was lost, he wanted his cavalry to live to fight another day.

Activities

1. Divide into two groups – one takes the Battle of Stirling, the other the Battle of Falkirk.
   a) Make a list of all the ways that *Braveheart's* account of the battle was incorrect.
   b) Looking only at what actually happened, make a list of facts which suggest that Wallace was a good general.
   c) Now make a list of facts which suggest that Wallace was actually *not* a very good general. Share your findings about your battle with someone who studied the other battle.
2. Look back at the headlines you wrote for the dates 11 September 1297 and 22 July 1298 (when you were pretending to be a Scottish newspaper editor, on page 25). In the light of what you have learned on pages 26–27, do you want to change your headlines?
   Think also: would the headlines have been any different if you had been an *English* newspaper editor?
3. Choose one battle and write the article to accompany your revised headline.

Representation: Images of Wallace

SOURCE 1

He was a tall man with the body of a giant, cheerful-looking with handsome features, broad-shouldered and big-boned, with long legs, good-looking but with a wild look, a most spirited fighting-man, with all his limbs very strong and firm.

Walter Bower, *Scotichronicon* (c.1450)

Bower was abbot of Inchcolm Monastery, and a very bad historian. We cannot trust this description of Wallace at all.

SOURCE 2

A poster for the film *Braveheart* (1995).

Mel Gibson, the director, said that he had wanted to make a 'swashbuckling' historical epic like *Spartacus* – such as he had seen in his childhood.

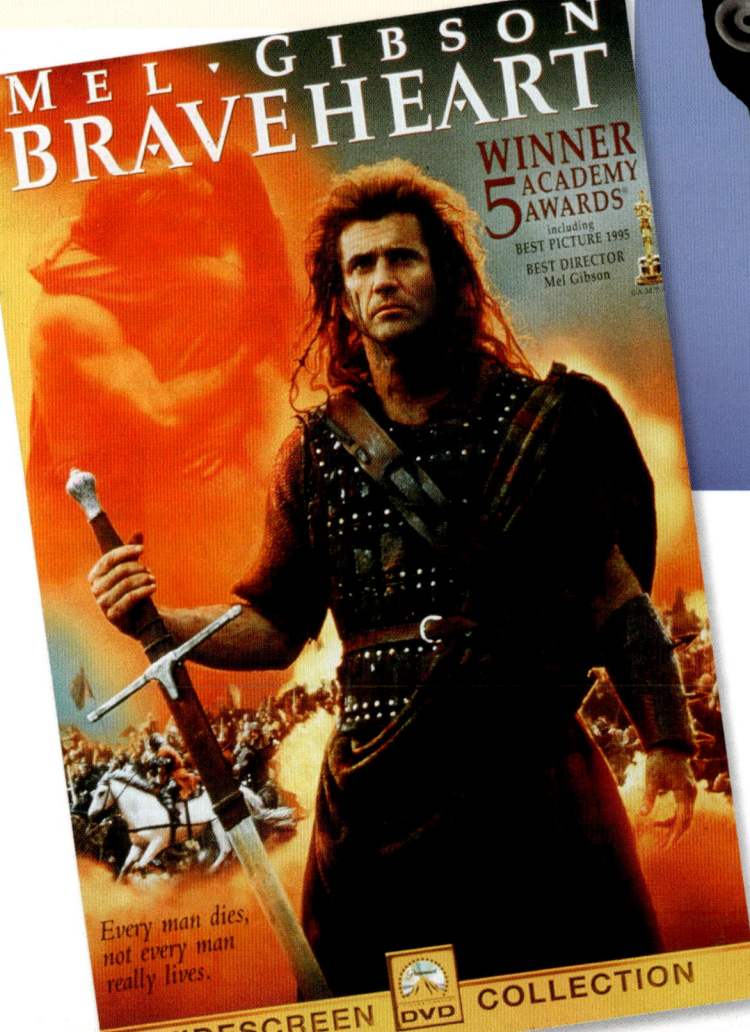

SOURCE 3

The Wallace monument in Aberdeen was erected in 1888.

The statue is 16 feet high and shows the moment in history when Wallace met the English before the battle of Stirling Bridge, and said: 'We came not to talk, but to fight and set Scotland free'.

The monument was built with money given by John Steill, a nationalist who was worried that the Scottish people were becoming weak.

SOURCE 4

This is an illustration drawn to accompany Jane Porter's best-selling novel *The Scottish Chiefs* (1809), a romantic and melodramatic story of Wallace's life.

SOURCE 5

An engraving made in 1757 for Smollett's *History of England*. Smollett was born in Scotland. He tried and failed to become a doctor, and served as a sailor, before becoming a writer of violent, racy novels. He loved Scottish history. His *History* was popular, and made him a fortune, but it was attacked for being merely a collection of exciting stories.

SOURCE 6

This print was drawn to accompany Robert Burns' nationalistic and romantic poem *Scots wha hae* (see page 41) in an edition of Burns' poems published in 1839.

It is said to show William Wallace leading the Scots against the English.

SOURCE 7

This drawing was done as a picture for a children's history book: *Heroes and Heroines of English History* (1914) by Alice S. Hoffman.

The artist, Gordon Browne, drew his characters to make history seem full of glamour, chivalry, adventure and bravery.

SOURCE 8

This modern painting of Wallace was specially drawn in 2005 to celebrate the 700th anniversary of Wallace's execution.

SOURCE 9

SOURCE 9

This drawing from the children's history book *Scotland's story: a history of Scotland for boys and girls* (1906) illustrates a story about Wallace being warned of a trap.

The author, HE Marshall, was a careful and balanced writer, and the artist has taken care to get the armour and clothing right for the time.

SOURCE 10

This iconic image from the film *Braveheart* (1995) shows Wallace with Princess Isabelle, just after she has warned him of a trap. It is interesting to compare this picture with Source 9.

Activities

Because we do not know what Wallace looked like, artists have portrayed him as they liked, making his appearance fit with their interpretation of what kind of person they thought he was.

1. Study Sources 2–10.
   a) For each representation of Wallace, explain what 'image of Wallace' they were trying to get across, and what makes you think this.

b) Choose the image you think best fits each of these 'Wallaces' – Wallace the: determined, kind, popular, romantic, suffering, superhuman, swashbuckling, victim, warrior.

2. Look at the provenance of all the illustrations 2–10. Which do you think is the most reliable source? Which is the least?

3. Which portrayal best fits your imagined image of Wallace? Explain why.

Using evidence: Edward's easy victory

How difficult did Edward I find it to conquer Scotland?
You will already have an idea of your own from your studies so far.
How far do the following sources from different historians match your own opinion?

SOURCE 1

'The English forces of King Edward I battle against the Scots under William Wallace' – a print by Joseph Kronheim in the children's history book *Pictures of English History* (c. 1870).

Kronheim was a German artist who worked as a printer in Edinburgh before settling in London in 1846.

SOURCE 2

In the following spring Edward marched north to teach the Scots a lesson. His army contained a strong force of archers armed with longbows. These deadly weapons, five or six feet high, could fire iron-tipped arrows through chain mail! Edward's archers quickly settled the issue at the battle of Falkirk (1298). Wallace fled into hiding, and the rebellion was broken, Edward, 'the Hammer of the Scots', now ruled Scotland through a council of nobles … In 1305 Wallace was captured, after seven years on the run.

RJ Cootes, *The Middle Ages* (1972)

This was a school textbook written for pupils aged 12 or 13, and it tried to be 'clear and simple'. Richard Cootes was a history teacher, and he wanted his book to be interesting.

SOURCE 3

Edward decided that he would come up personally to Scotland with the largest army he could get. One report claims that there were a whopping 87,000 men in it … There were many hundreds of armoured knights on great big battle horses. And there were thousands of foot-soldiers and archers – all armed to the teeth …

Wallace only had about 8,000 in his army, possibly far fewer. For Wallace and his men, taking on Longshanks' horde was like one football team trying to play against at least two others at the same time …

Eventually the sheer size of the English army began to crush the Scots like an elephant rolling over a mouse.

Allan Burnett, *William Wallace and all that* (2006)

This book claims to be 'blood-spattered Scottish history at its most wickedly entertaining'. The author writes: 'This book contains a lot of facts about Wallace's life, as well as many traditional Wallace stories and legends which may or may not be true'.

SOURCE 4

Edward mangled the Scots at the battle of Falkirk in 1298.

Mary R Price, *A Portrait of Britain in the Middle Ages* (1951)

This school textbook was written by a teacher, and was intended to prepare pupils for the GCE exam.

SOURCE 5

As none of the Scots would resist, nothing glorious or even worthy of praise was achieved.

The comment of an English chronicler on Edward's campaign of 1301.

Activities

1. Study Source 1. What impression does it give of Edward's army? What impression does it give of the Scots?
2. Make a list of factors that might lead to one army defeating another army. Choose the THREE most important.
3. Read Sources 2 and 3. Make a list of all the factors which meant that Edward defeated the Scots.
4. Read Sources 2–5. For each, explain how it gives the impression that Edward's victory was easy.

Knowledge: Edward's 'easy' victory revisited

The truth is that Edward found the conquest of Scotland anything BUT easy.

Did Edward conquer the Scots at Falkirk?

Absolutely not!

Although Edward turned out a much bigger army than the Scots, and defeated them in the pitched battle at Falkirk, he could not afford to *keep* a standing army in the field.

The Scots reacted to this simply by refusing to take on Edward's army in battle. And as soon as Edward's army had gone away, the Scots moved back in and took over again. Before 1302, the English were only in control in a number of castles they held. And if you look at the map (right), you will see that they controlled precious few castles. The English sheriffs did not manage to collect ANY taxes from Scotland before 1302, showing how little Edward actually *ruled* Scotland.

Edward's army did not get north of Stirling until 1303. For the period 1297–1304 Scotland was ruled by Scottish nobles and Parliament.

Was Edward stronger than the Scots during the wars?

Arguably, and surprisingly, probably not!

After the battle of Falkirk, the Scots used 'hit-and-run' tactics. When the English went out to meet them, the Scots retreated. Edward could not get enough 'hobelars' (foot-soldiers with horses) who could chase them as they ran away. And royal documents show that Edward also had great difficulty transporting the siege engines he needed to capture the Scottish castles.

The English people did not support the war with Scotland, and they tried everything to get out of fighting. In October 1297 Edward summoned 30,000 soldiers to attack Scotland; only 7,000 turned up, and Edward was forced to abandon the campaign.

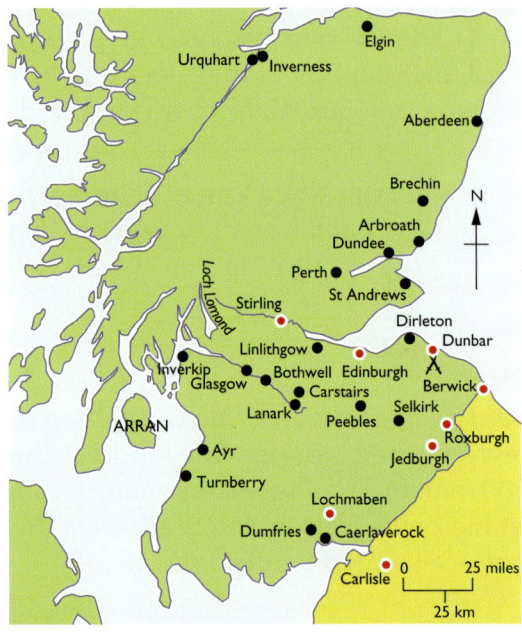

1298 When Edward left Scotland the English presence in Scotland amounted to only a few castles (shown by ◉), and Lochmaben and Stirling were in great difficulties. The Scots government ran the country; in 1299 they met at Peebles.

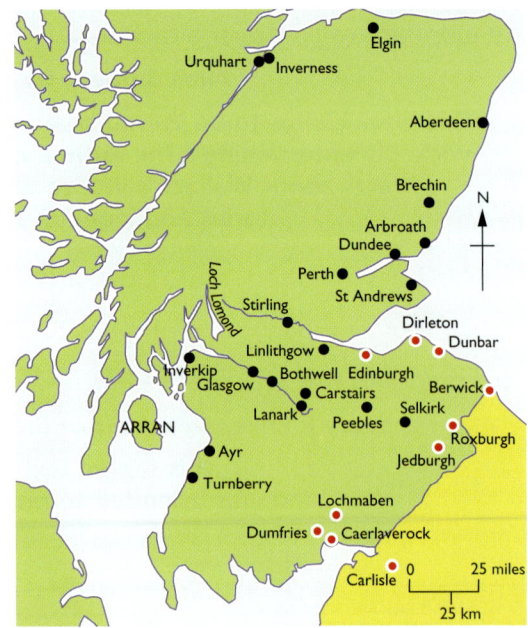

1300 Despite fresh campaigns in 1299 and 1300, Edward had made very little progress, capturing only a few more castles. Outside the castle walls, the Scots ruled the land; in 1300 they called a Parliament at Rutherglen, near Glasgow.

Edward and the crisis of 1297

Edward almost lost power in 1297, when he was trying to raise armies to fight in France *and* Scotland.

The Church refused to pay any more taxes and the nobles refused to fight.

In July, in tears, Edward I begged people's forgiveness and promised to put things right.

But when he carried on raising his armies, the barons began to get ready for a civil war.

Ironically, William Wallace saved Edward from a rebellion which might have knocked him off the throne: the Scottish victory at Stirling Bridge angered the English so much that they stopped their rebellion and helped Edward.

Instead, Edward had to PAY his soldiers to fight, unlike the Scots, who could still call up their men to fight for 40 days for free as part of their 'service' for their land. Consequently, Edward was always desperate for money to pay for his soldiers. In 1301, the soldiers at Berwick Castle went on strike because they had not been paid.

Edward's policy of buying his supplies meant that he was also continually short of food. During the Falkirk campaign of 1298 some of his soldiers died of starvation, and he was about to retreat back home when William Wallace saved his campaign by offering – and losing – the battle at Falkirk.

In 1303 the Scots sent two messengers to surrender to Edward. But when they saw the poverty-stricken, starving state of Edward's soldiers, they changed their minds and carried on fighting!

Activities

1. Why did Edward find it so difficult to subdue Scotland when his army was so big?
2. Using your 'list of factors that might lead to one army defeating another army' from page 33, use pages 34–35 to explain why Edward found it so difficult to conquer Scotland.
3. Use the maps to prove that Edward found it very difficult to subdue Scotland.
4. So ... why didn't the Scots win the war?

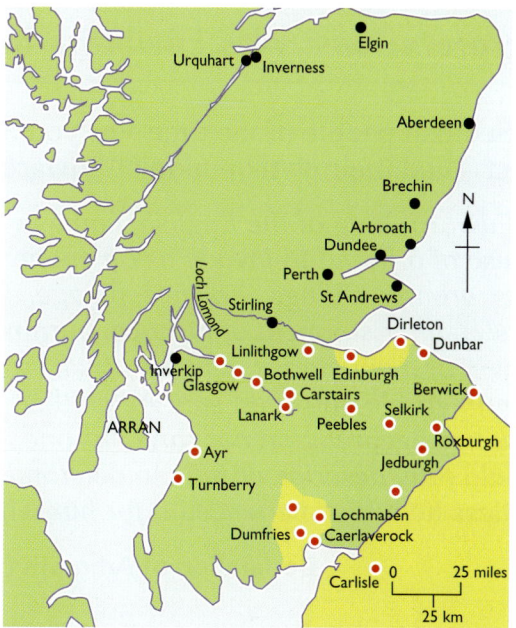

1301 Edward's 1301 campaign made better progress. At the same time he ordered his officials to attract the 'middle sort' of Scots to his side with fair government and good laws.
For the first time, English officials managed to collect taxes from the areas around some of their castles (shown in yellow).

1303 Edward used a truce in 1302 to get control over the Lowlands. In 1303, although part of his army was defeated by a Scots ambush at Rosslyn, he was able to advance into the Highlands (the route ——).
1304 The Scots surrendered.

Interpretations: Was Edward a bad man?

The Scottish people of the time – as you might expect – had their own opinion of Edward I.

'Edward, king of the English, came in the guise of a friend to invade as an enemy. His wrongs, killings, violence, pillage, arson, imprisonment of bishops, burning down of monasteries, and yet other innumerable outrages, sparing neither sex nor age, religion nor rank, no-one could fully describe or fully understand unless he had experienced it for himself.'

Declaration of Arbroath (1320)

This spread will help you to form your own opinion of Edward I.

1 Edward believed that justice made a government safe from rebellion. He made laws to stop crime and punish rapists, and made landowners prove they owned their land.

2 In 1304, when the defenders of Stirling Castle surrendered, Edward refused to accept their surrender until he had tried out a new siege engine.

3 In 1306, Edward set up 'Commissions of Trailbaston' (named after the great clubs the investigators carried) to smash the power of local gangsters in the towns.

4 When a laundress complained in 1289 that a judge had cheated her, Edward investigated and found his judges *were* corrupt. He fined many of them, and sent one to the Tower.

5 Edward conquered Wales – he starved the Welsh armies into defeat and built many huge castles.

Edward I – the judgement of historians

Historians have had different ideas ('interpretations') about Edward:

a. **Michael Prestwich** of Durham University says he was: 'the most respected prince in Europe'.
b. **Fiona Watson** from the University of Stirling says that: 'the ability to learn, adapt and compromise – always with an eye on the main prize in the long run – was what defined Edward's greatness'.
c. **Allan Burnett**, the children's writer, says that: 'He was a scheming villain'.
d. **Duncan MacGillivray**, writer of a children's textbook (1923), said: 'Great as he was as a warrior, he was just as great as a lawgiver'.
e. **Richard Cootes**, writer of a children's textbook (1972), called him: 'A wise and firm ruler, who was also an outstanding soldier and more religious than most medieval kings'.

6 In 1295, Edward held the 'Model Parliament' – the first *real* Parliament (because it invited people from the towns and counties as well as nobles and bishops).

7 Edward held 'round table' meetings of his nobles. In 1306, at a lavish knighting ceremony for his son, Edward 'swore on the swans' – a very holy oath – to conquer Scotland.

8 In 1290 Edward expelled all the Jews from England. (In the Middle Ages, many people hated the Jews.)

9 Edward once sent ambassadors to the Mongol Khan in Central Asia (they came back with the first umbrellas ever seen in England).

10 When Edward's favourite falcon was ill, he ordered that a wax model of the bird should be placed in Canterbury Cathedral.

11 Edward fought at the battle of Falkirk despite two broken ribs; and at the siege of Stirling in 1304 he had his horse killed under him.

12 When Edward wrote to the people of Nottingham that he was coming to stay, he added a sentence promising he would not stay long.

13 Records show that Edward once paid 20 marks to say sorry to a page whom he hit on the head in a fit of temper.

14 In 1306 Edward ordered royal officials to arrest an MP who had criticised him five years earlier.

15 The King of Cyprus asked Edward to be judge in a dispute between him and his barons.

16 Edward held investigations in 1298 and 1300 to make sure that government officials weren't cheating the people.

17 Edward once left a letter on his bed containing false information, knowing that his second wife Margaret would read it and tell her brother Philip IV of France what it said.

A picture of Edward I, his clerks and his court in a Book of Psalms from *c.* 1290.

18 In 1306, Edward put the Countess of Buchan – who had helped the Scottish rebels – in a cage in Berwick castle (although he gave her a private latrine).

19 During his wars with Scotland, Edward ordered his officers to appeal to the 'middle sort' of Scots and he tried to be a good ruler, so that ordinary people would leave the Scottish side.

20 During his wars with Scotland, Edward *bought* his armies' supplies, sometimes from Scottish merchants. He upheld Scottish laws and punished English officials who harmed Scottish people.

Activities

Historians have had different ideas ('interpretations') about Edward.

1. Read the twenty statements on pages 36–37. For each historian a–e, find TWO facts that they might use to support their ideas. Can you find a fact that seems to contradict their ideas?
2. Read all twenty statements. What is YOUR interpretation of Edward? Find two facts to support YOUR ideas.

Knowledge: The death of Wallace

As the Scottish war effort fell apart in 1304, Wallace tried to surrender, but Edward refused. Soon after, in August 1305, Wallace was captured by Sir John of Monteith (who has been hated ever since).

Wallace was taken to London and put on trial, charged with a long list of offences. 'The charges brought against him can also be read as a list of his achievements' writes historian Fiona Watson. In those days, the list of offences was taken as proof of guilt, and he was not allowed to defend himself. Wallace argued that he could not be guilty of treason, because Edward I was not his king – John Balliol was his king. But he was ignored.

On 23 August, Wallace was sentenced to be hanged, then cut down, beheaded, his heart, liver and lungs burned, his body cut into four parts (to be sent to Newcastle, Berwick, Stirling and Perth), and his head set up on London Bridge 'in the sight of such as pass by'. He was dragged to Smithfield behind horses' tails, and the sentence was carried out.

Charges brought against Wallace

That he had:
- rebelled against his lord King
- attacked the king's officers and soldiers
- killed William de Hazelrig, cutting his body in pieces
- made laws and called Parliaments, as if he were ruler of Scotland
- made an alliance with the king of France, and helped France to destroy England
- invaded the north of England, committing horrible atrocities
- killed men loyal to the king
- killed people who spoke English
- killed old and young, wives and widows, children and sucklings
- killed priests and nuns and burned down churches
- rebelliously and wickedly refused to submit when the Lord King invaded Scotland and graciously offered his peace
- been declared an outlaw and a robber.

SOURCE 1

He is Wallace, defender of Scotland,
For righteous war that he took upon hand.
On Wednesday the false Southerons brought him forth
To martyr him, as they had planned before.

Blind Harry, *The Wallace* (c. 1475)

SOURCE 2

Sir John of Mentieth in those days
Took in Glasgow Willam Walays,
And sent him into England soon:
There was he quartered and undone
By hatred and hot envy:
There he suffered his martyry.

Andrew of Wyntoun, *The Origynale Cronykil of Scotland* (1420)

SOURCE 3

Butcher of thousands, threefold death be yours
So shall the English from thee gain relief
Scotland, be wise, and choose a nobler chief.

***Chronicle of Lanercost* (c. 1350)**

Lanercost was an English monastery on the Scottish border – although the Chronicle was probably not written by a monk from Lanercost, but by a monk from nearby Carlisle.

SOURCE 4

The Trial of Wallace, a painting by William Bell Scott.

William Bell Scott (1811–90) was born in Edinburgh, and became head of the School of Design at Newcastle.

Activities

1. 'The charges brought against him can also be read as a list of his achievements'. Explain what Fiona Watson meant when she wrote this.
2. How – and why – do Sources 1 and 2 differ from Source 3?
3. Both Harry and Wyntoun describe Wallace's death as a 'martyrdom'. Look at Source 4. Find all the ways the artist picks up the theme of martyrdom and portrays the scene as a religious persecution.
4. Look at all the sources and write your own four-line poem about the death of Wallace.

SOURCE 5

The plaque to William Wallace at Smithfield.

The Latin phrase – which Wallace may have said at his trial – means: 'My Son, I tell you the truth: freedom is the best of things. Never live under the bonds of slavery.'

Bas Agus Buaidh is a Gaelic phrase meaning: 'Death and Victory'.

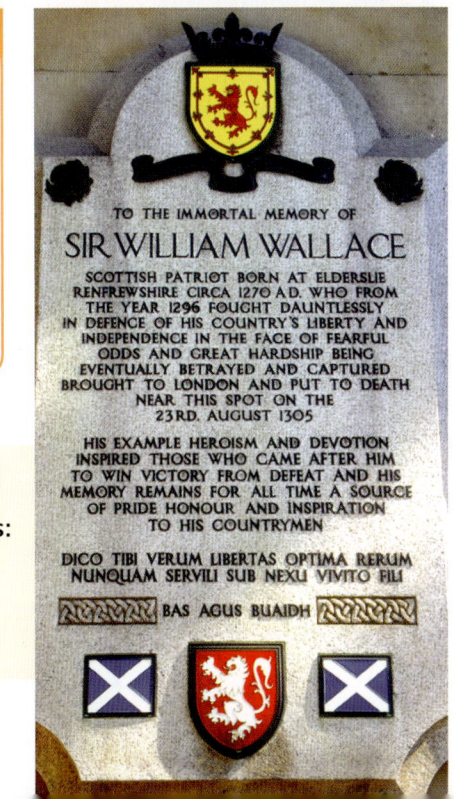

TO THE IMMORTAL MEMORY OF
SIR WILLIAM WALLACE
SCOTTISH PATRIOT BORN AT ELDERSLIE
RENFREWSHIRE CIRCA 1270 A.D. WHO FROM
THE YEAR 1296 FOUGHT DAUNTLESSLY
IN DEFENCE OF HIS COUNTRY'S LIBERTY AND
INDEPENDENCE IN THE FACE OF FEARFUL
ODDS AND GREAT HARDSHIP BEING
EVENTUALLY BETRAYED AND CAPTURED
BROUGHT TO LONDON AND PUT TO DEATH
NEAR THIS SPOT ON THE
23RD. AUGUST 1305

HIS EXAMPLE HEROISM AND DEVOTION
INSPIRED THOSE WHO CAME AFTER HIM
TO WIN VICTORY FROM DEFEAT AND HIS
MEMORY REMAINS FOR ALL TIME A SOURCE
OF PRIDE HONOUR AND INSPIRATION
TO HIS COUNTRYMEN

DICO TIBI VERUM LIBERTAS OPTIMA RERUM
NUNQUAM SERVILI SUB NEXU VIVITO FILI

BAS AGUS BUAIDH

CHAPTER 5

After Braveheart

Interpretations: Wallace keeps on running

What is a 'nation'?

Historians tell us that, before 1300, medieval people did not have a sense of 'nation'. They called themselves 'Scottis' or 'Inglis', but their loyalty – their 'homage' – was to a KING, not to an abstract idea called 'a nation'.

But in 1320, in an appeal to the Pope called 'The Declaration of Arbroath', the Scottish people showed that they certainly DID have a sense of nation:

> 'If our king should seek to make us or our kingdom subject to the English, we would strive to drive him out as our enemy, and we would make some other man our king. For as long as a hundred men remain alive, we shall never accept English rule. It is not for glory or riches that we are fighting, but for freedom. '

It is the most amazing document. It changes our ideas about Scotland in the Middle Ages.

An amazing and wonderful thing had happened in the sixteen years that Scotland had been without a king (1286–92 and 1296–1306), and the eighteen years of war with England (1296–1314). The Scots had discovered their identity as a nation, which they were now calling 'our kingdom'. And their loyalty now was to 'Scotland', and not to whoever sat on the throne.

Robert the Bruce

In 1305 Edward I left Scotland. This time he left Scottish people in charge of the government there.

His triumph did not last long. In 1306 Robert Bruce declared himself king, and Scotland was plunged into war again.

Eight years later, in 1314, the Scots defeated the English at Bannockburn, and in 1328 Edward III of England recognised Scotland as an independent country with its own king.

And it was not the last time people would hear of William Wallace.

This painting, by William Bell Scott, shows Edward marching to war against Bruce in 1307. The king, knowing that he was dying, ordered that he be carried at the front of his army.

There are many legends in northern Europe about 'sleeping warriors', who do not die, but who lie asleep, ready to return if their country is ever in danger. William Wallace is Scotland's version of the legend of the sleeping warrior, as from time to time in history he has been brought out to inspire and save the Scottish nation.

Blind Harry and his followers

In the 1470s, James III was king of Scotland. James was a weak king, dominated by the English. It was at this time that 'Blind Harry' wrote *The Wallace*, a collection of all the stories and legends that had grown up about Wallace in the years since his death. The Scottish nobles used the poem as propaganda to oppose James III's alliances with England.

In 1570 Scotland was in danger again. The Queen of Scotland was the unstable Mary Queen of Scots, and by 1568 Mary was a prisoner in an English castle. It was at this time that Robert Lekpreuik, an Edinburgh printer, re-published Blind Harry's poem. Lekpreuik edited the poem so it was acceptable to the Protestant Scots of the time, and he re-organised it into twelve books, to make it more readable.

In 1603 King James VI of Scotland became also King James I of England, and in 1707 the two countries were officially united by the Act of Union. In 1715 there was a failed rebellion in Scotland, after which General Wade went north to keep the Scots under control. In 1722, Hamilton of Gilbertfield, a Scottish poet, modernised and translated *The Wallace* for the Scottish readers of the time.

One of the Scots who read the new edition was Robert Burns, the great Scots poet, who said that it: 'poured a Scottish prejudice in my veins, which will boil along there till the flood-gates of life shut in eternal rest', and inspired him to write the poem *Bannockburn*.

SOURCE 1

Bannockburn
Robert Bruce's address to his army

> Scots, wha hae wi' Wallace bled,
> Scots, wham Bruce has aften led,
> Welcome to your gory bed,
> Or to Victorie!
> Now's the day, and now's the hour:
> See the front o' battle lour,
> See approach proud Edward's power –
> Chains and Slaverie!
> Wha will be a traitor knave?
> Wha will fill a coward's grave?
> Wha sae base as be a slave?
> Let him turn and flee!
> Wha, for Scotland's King and Law,
> Freedom's sword will strongly draw,
> Freeman stand, or Freeman fa',
> Let him on wi' me!
> By Oppression's woes and pains!
> By your sons in servile chains!
> We will drain our dearest veins,
> But they shall be free!
> Lay the proud usurpers low!
> Tyrants fall in every foe!
> Liberty's in every blow! –
> Let us do or die!

Robert Burns (1793)

Burns admitted that he took the lines at the end directly from Gilbertfield's edition of Blind Harry: 'A false usurper sinks in every foe, And liberty returns with every blow'.

A Wallace for all seasons

Over the succeeding years, the Scots have reinvented Wallace in different images.

Romantic Wallace

In the nineteenth century Scotland was prosperous and happy, and many Scots emigrated to live all over the world. During this time of displacement, the Wallace story was re-interpreted for the industrial age by Jane Porter in her novel *The Scottish Chiefs*, which was full of adventure, melodrama and romance.

Porter's heroic story of William Wallace helped to keep Scottish identity and Scottish pride alive. The great Scottish-American businessman Andrew Carnegie always said that it was Wallace who had made him proud of being Scottish, and claimed that in difficult moments of decision in his life he would ask himself: 'What would Wallace have done?'

Working-class Wallace

As Scotland grew into the twentieth century, Wallace was recruited for another campaign: the cause of the working man.

Scottish working-class leaders made much of the fact that it was the ordinary poor men of Scotland who had fought for Wallace, and 'developed, on the battlefield, a consciousness that they were equals of the knights and nobles they were fighting alongside. (Nay, 'betters' surely, for didn't the nobles betray and sell out Scotland time after time?)'

It is not true, of course – it is a case of reading back into history something that wasn't there at the time. In 1300, the Scottish peasants were as far politically from democracy as they were technologically from the machine-gun. But the film *Braveheart* picked up on the idea, showing Wallace as 'one of the lads', and portraying the nobles as self-seeking, bickering cowards.

SOURCE 2

'Marion!' burst from the overflowing soul of her fond husband. She looked up at the well-known sound, and with a cry of joy rushed forward and threw herself into his arms; her tears flowed, she sobbed – she clung to his breast.

'Art thou indeed here?' exclaimed she – Blood fell from his forehead upon her face and bosom: 'O my Wallace, my Wallace,' cried she, in an agony clasping him to her heart.

'Fear not my love! It is a mere scratch ... '

Jane Porter, *The Scottish Chiefs* (1809)

In Porter's book, Wallace is not executed at all, but dies beautifully – his loved one in his arms – before the executioner could put the noose over his head.

Activities

1. Explain how 'William Wallace is Scotland's version of the legend of the sleeping warrior'.
2. Explain how different generations of Scots have 'reinvented Wallace in different images'.
3. Read all the information on pages 42–43, and write a short passage: 'What does Wallace mean for Scots today?'
4. Now write a more personal passage: 'What Wallace means to *me*'.

Nationalist Wallace

The other modern battle, of course, that Wallace has found himself fighting in, is the battle over Scottish independence. For more than a century, many Scots have wanted independence, and it is understandable why Wallace is their hero. Every year the Scottish National Party hold a march to Elderslie, one of Wallace's possible birthplaces, and it is widely believed that the success of *Braveheart* helped get a 'Yes' vote for a Scottish Parliament in 1997.

Tourist attraction Wallace

Also, since even before *Braveheart*, but especially after, Wallace has become a great tourist attraction. You can go on the Wallace Heritage Trail, and visit Wallace monuments and museums, and buy Wallace souvenirs. In the year 2000, around 200,000 people visited the National Wallace Monument at Stirling.

After watching *Braveheart*, a stonemason called Tom Church was inspired to make a statue of Wallace looking like Mel Gibson!
It was placed in the car park of the National Monument.
Although the Scots loved Mel Gibson as *Braveheart* in the film, they were less than happy with the statue, and after someone attacked it with a hammer, the statue had to be protected by a mesh cage – the ultimate irony, given the kind of person Wallace was, and the word 'Freedom' on the base.

Statements made on the 700th anniversary of Wallace's execution ...

In my view, the best tribute to William Wallace would be for Scotland to regain the Independence that he fought and died for.
Nicola Sturgeon, Leader of the Scottish National Party Group in the Scottish Parliament

Wallace proved that anyone has the potential to be a leader and make a difference.
Colin Fox, Member of the Scottish Parliament

We need uncompromising heroes like Wallace: heroes that remind us what is important about life.
Lin Anderson, author of *Braveheart – Hollywood to Holyrood*

Seven hundred years on and William Wallace still has the establishment scared stiff.
Alex Salmond, Leader of the Scottish Nationalist Party

... and some comments on the Internet

I am a Christian, and Braveheart has special meaning for me. Living from the heart, like Wallace did ... that is what God intended for us.

Mel Gibson is a dish, but how can any woman not fall in love with the real William Wallace?
Whenever I am sad or down I watch *Braveheart* and a strange pride and happiness comes to me, even though it's not my country's tale. The movie has taught me to feel proud for my beliefs.

William Wallace is an important person in my life because he is a great role model. He believed in freedom and rights for all people and stood by it.

#########FFFRRREEEDDDOOOMMM######

Interpretations: Scotland's greatest hero?

Yes but, no but

Who are the other contenders?

Scotland's genius poet (d.1796) wrote 'Auld Lang Syne'. A nationalist, his poems made the Scottish dialect as a valid form of literature. Burns night (25 January) is celebrated all over the world.

1 **Robert Burns**

Guardian of Scotland for a year. Won a battle but lost the war. Failed to unite the Scots. Captured and executed in 1305.

2 **William Wallace**

Developed the steam engine (1765) and thereby basically caused the Industrial Revolution. Also a successful businessman.

3 **James Watt**

Beat the English at Bannockburn, 1314, and drove them out of Scotland. Became king (1306–29); founder of a dynasty.

4 **Robert Bruce**

Led the 1745 rebellion. Won more than one battle, and invaded England. He reached Derby before turning back to Scotland, where he was defeated in 1746. The hero still of songs such as 'Charlie is my Darling'.

5 **Bonnie Prince Charlie**

Activity

Debate as a whole class: Who do you think was Scotland's greatest hero?

Selfless missionary who spent his adulthood in Africa. Explorer and geographer who discovered Victoria Falls and mapped central Africa. Campaigned against the slave trade. Has a town in Zambia named after him.

6 David Livingstone

Scottish bacteriologist who in 1928 discovered penicillin, which for the first time enabled doctors to defeat infectious diseases.

7 Alexander Fleming

Missionary, who went to Nigeria in 1876. Persuaded the chiefs to end the burning of widows and the killing of twins, and set up churches, schools and hospitals.

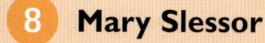

8 Mary Slessor

Went to Australia as a child in 1839. A great feminist – Australia's first female political candidate and first woman journalist. Sometimes called 'Australia's greatest woman'. There is a statue to her in Adelaide.

9 Catherine Spence

Starting from nothing, he built up a huge steel business in America. Gave $ millions to libraries and universities. Set up the Carnegie Endowment for International Peace, and funded Carnegie Hall in New York.

10 Andrew Carnegie

Debate: What they have said about William Wallace ...

Arguments FOR William Wallace

1 Wallace started it all – started the Wars of Independence, started Scottish national identity – when he started the rebellion in 1297. He was the first Scot who believed in Scotland.

2 Wallace went to France to seek help; he developed the 'auld alliance' with France, which became a main policy of Scotland's kings.

3 Wallace became 'Guardian' of Scotland – its war leader. He showed that determination and strong leadership could hold up the unstoppable juggernaut of Edward's bigger, more modern army, and he even beat it at Stirling Bridge.

4 Like only the most forward-thinking people of the time, Wallace knew the importance of trade, and that's why he wrote to the merchants of Lübeck in 1297.

5 He was NOT a noble. He was the first person from his social class to have an impact on Scotland's affairs.

6 He re-organised the army and invented conscription, forcing thousands of 'the common folk' to join his army.

7 He invented the guerrilla tactics that held the English tyrants at bay. Future Scottish leaders just copied him.

8 Wallace didn't fail. He was betrayed by the nobles, who regarded him as an upstart; he would have won if they hadn't sold out to Edward.

9 Wallace died a hero's death after an unfair trial; he is a Scottish martyr.

10 Wallace has been an example and a figurehead for Scots from the time and ever since – an inspiration whenever Scotland has been in danger. His cry for 'FREEDOM!' was an inspiration for Robert Burns, and it still inspires people all over the world today.

Activities – Debate

1. Divide into two groups, 'for' and 'against' William Wallace. Working with a friend, discuss the ideas on pages 46–47 that support 'your' case. Try to find, in this book, facts that prove the points.

2. Looking back through the book, think of some other points to make about whether William was a great hero or not.

3. Coming together as a whole class, debate the idea: Does William Wallace deserve to be Scotland's hero?
   Does your opinion depend on whether you regard yourself as 'Scottish' or 'English'?

Arguments AGAINST William Wallace

1 He can't be your hero, because you know so little about him.

2 Wallace didn't start it all. He was a petty thief and outlaw who was used as a figurehead by the nobles until he lost a battle – then they dumped him and took over.

3 We would find Wallace far too violent today, and his idea of 'Scotland' is not appropriate for the modern world.

4 Wallace did not invent 'the auld alliance': Balliol and the Guardians did that in 1295, before Wallace appeared.

5 Wallace was a useless general. It was Moray who won at Stirling Bridge. And if Wallace had left Edward alone in 1298, the English invasion would have fizzled out; instead he chose to fight a pitched battle at Falkirk he was bound to lose!

6 In 1297 Edward was about to lose his throne – by winning at Stirling Bridge, Wallace kept Edward in power!

7 Wallace tried to beat Edward by a 'scorched earth' policy – by killing and starving his own people. It was Edward who bought his own supplies and gave law and good government; that was one of the reasons why Edward won in the end.

8 We know now that Edward's task in conquering Scotland was much harder than people thought; beating the English wasn't impossible – Bruce proved that in 1314.

9 The nobles did not betray Scotland. Red Comyn led the Scots army for six years after Wallace resigned; it was he who developed the hit-and-run tactics that held back Edward.

10 'Wallace' is just a creation of the Scottish propaganda machine – a series of made-up stories.

Activities – Summing it all up

1. On page 5, at the beginning of this course, you were asked to suggest a caption for this photograph. Look back at what you wrote. At the end of the course, do you still feel that your caption was appropriate? Think of a new, better-informed caption.
2. On page 4 you were also asked to write down your 'First thoughts' about William Wallace. Look back at what you wrote. At the end of the course, do you still agree with what you wrote?
3. If you had to sum up your thoughts about William Wallace now, what would you say? Write down your new, better-informed ideas in less than 50 words.

Understanding: How significant was William Wallace?

On 23 August 2005, hundreds of people joined the historian David Ross (who had walked all the way from Glasgow) to Wallace's place of execution at Smithfield, and held a memorial service.

Significance involves five ideas. We might say William Wallace is significant if:

1 **His story tells you a lot about history.**
How much have you learned about Scotland and England by studying William Wallace? Scan back through the book and select TWO important facts you have learned.

2 **He had a big effect.**
Search back through the book (especially pages 28–31, 39 and 40–42) looking for the effects of Wallace's life. Choose TWO results you feel were especially important.

3 **He was important at the time.**
Scan back through the book (especially pages 24–27 and 38). Find TWO good examples of facts or sources which give the impression that people *at the time* thought that Wallace was important.

4 **People still remember him.**
I suppose the fact that you are studying him now proves they do! But how widely remembered is William Wallace? Find TWO clues from pages 4–5, 6–10, 43 or 48.

5 **His story means something today.**
Scan back through the book and find TWO issues that the story of William Wallace raised in your mind. Discuss with the class or a friend how relevant these issues are to us, in our world, today.

Activities – How significant was William Wallace?

1. How are the marchers in the picture showing they think William Wallace is still important today?
2. Using the ideas and information from this page, have a class discussion about how significant an historical character William Wallace was.
3. Have you ENJOYED studying William Wallace?